Patterns

Peter Patilla

First published in Great Britain by Heinemann Library,
Halley Court, Jordan Hill, Oxford OX2 8EJ,
a division of Reed Educational and Professional Publishing Ltd.
Heinemann is a registered trademark of Reed Educational & Professional Publishing Limited.

OXFORD MELBOURNE AUCKLAND
JOHANNESBURG BLANTYRE GABORONE
IBADAN PORTSMOUTH NH (USA) CHICAGO

Designed by AMR
Illustrations by Art Construction and Jessica Stockham (Beehive Illustration)
Originated by HBM Print Ltd, Singapore
Printed and bound by South China Printing Co., Hong Kong/China

03 02 01 00 99
10 9 8 7 6 5 4 3 2 1

ISBN 0 431 09356 3
British Library Cataloguing in Publication Data
Patilla, Peter
Patterns. – (Maths links)
I.Pattern perception – Juvenile literature 2.Geometrical constructions – Juvenile literature
I.Title.
516.1·5

Acknowledgements
The Publishers would like to thank the following for permission to reproduce photographs:
Trevor Clifford, pgs 8, 15, 17, 22, 24, 25, 26, 28; Bruce Coleman Ltd, pgs 4 /Luiz Claudio Marigo, 27 /Kim Taylor, 29 /Dr Stephen Coyne; Oxford Scientific Films, pg 6 /F. J. Hiersche/Okapia; Science Photo Library, pgs 7 /Adam Hart-Davis,11 /Peter Menzel, 21 /Martin Dohrn; Stockfile, pg 18 /Steven Behr; Tony Stone Images, pgs 10 /David Sutherland, 13 /Jean Francoise Causse.

Cover photograph reproduced with permission of Trevor Clifford.

Our thanks to David Kirkby for his comments in the preparation of this book.

For more information about Heinemann Library books, or to order, please phone +44 (0)1865 888066, or send a fax to +44 (0)1865 314091. You can visit our website at www.heinemann.co.uk

Contents

Some words are shown in bold, **like this**. You can find out what they mean by looking in the Glossary.

Animal patterns

Some animals have special patterns on them. These patterns are often stripes or spots. The colours and shapes of the pattern are very important. They **camouflage** the animal.

An animal with camouflage is difficult to see against its background. Animal patterns help them to hide in long grass, or against stones.

Which animals do you think have the patterns shown in the picture?

Nature's patterns

Patterns can be seen all around us. They can be found on seashells, flowers and birds. The patterns can be in the colour, shape or texture. Nature has many wonderful patterns.

Plants have different kinds of patterns in them. The veins on a leaf make a pattern. The pattern helps us to know which tree it came from.

Look at the leaves. Which leaves do you think came from the same tree?

Printed patterns

Patterns can be made by printing. This is where a pattern is copied from one place to another. Fingerprint patterns are **unique**. Every person in the world has a different pattern.

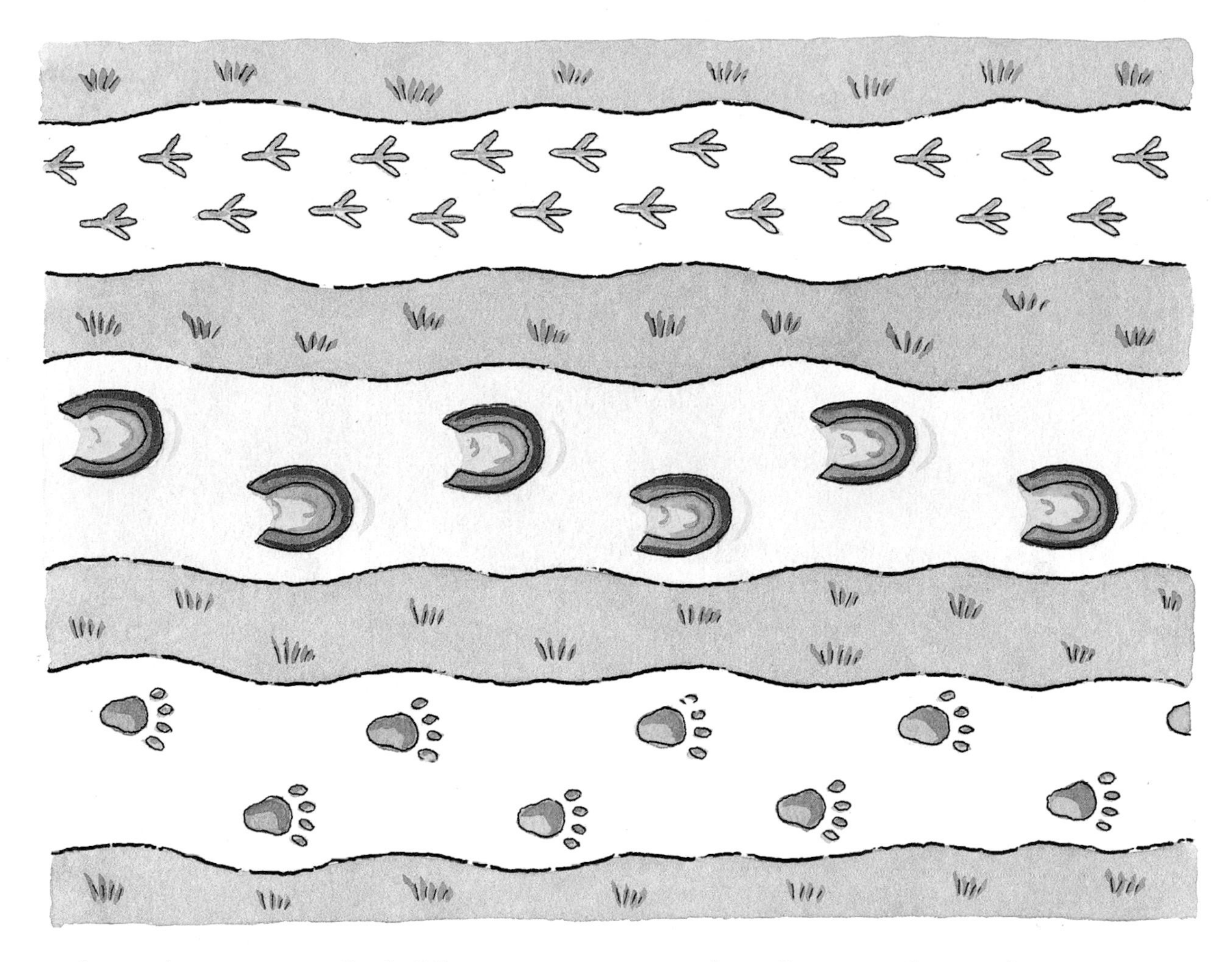

The shapes of different animals' feet often leave patterns on the ground. These footprint patterns can help us to identify the animal.

Which three animals do you think made the footprint patterns in the picture?

Colour patterns

Patterns can have colours in them. Sometimes the pattern has different shades of one colour, such as light red and dark red. We call these different **tints** or **hues** of red.

The rainbow makes a well-known pattern of seven colours. The colours are red, orange, yellow, green, blue, indigo and violet. One colour gently melts into the next.

Look at the picture of a rainbow. Can you find each colour?

Line patterns

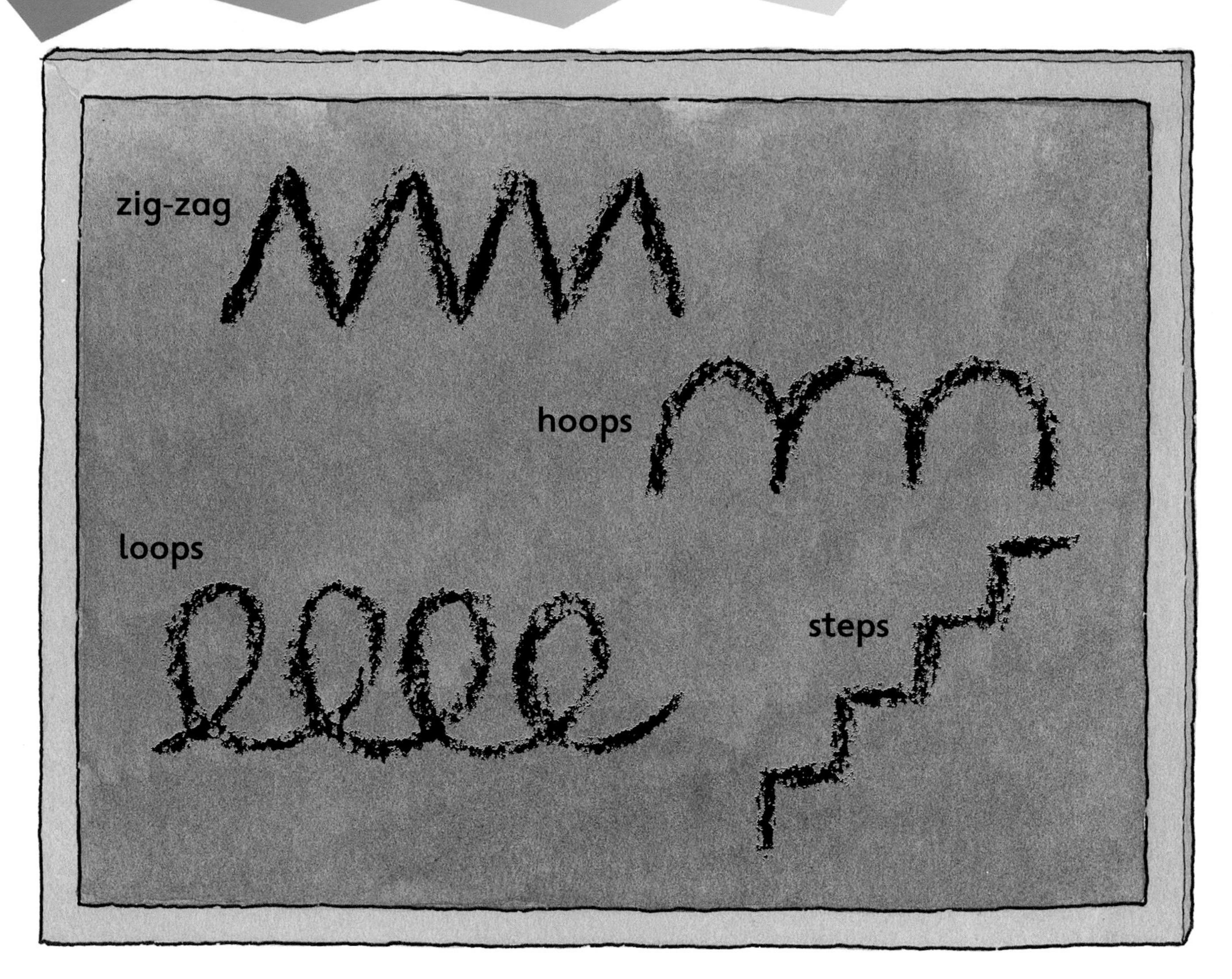

Lines can be drawn to make patterns. The lines can be straight or **curved**. There are **zig-zag** patterns, steps, loops and hoops.

Line patterns can be found all around us. Sometimes they are made by people, other times by animals or nature.

Look for the line patterns in the picture.

Spirals

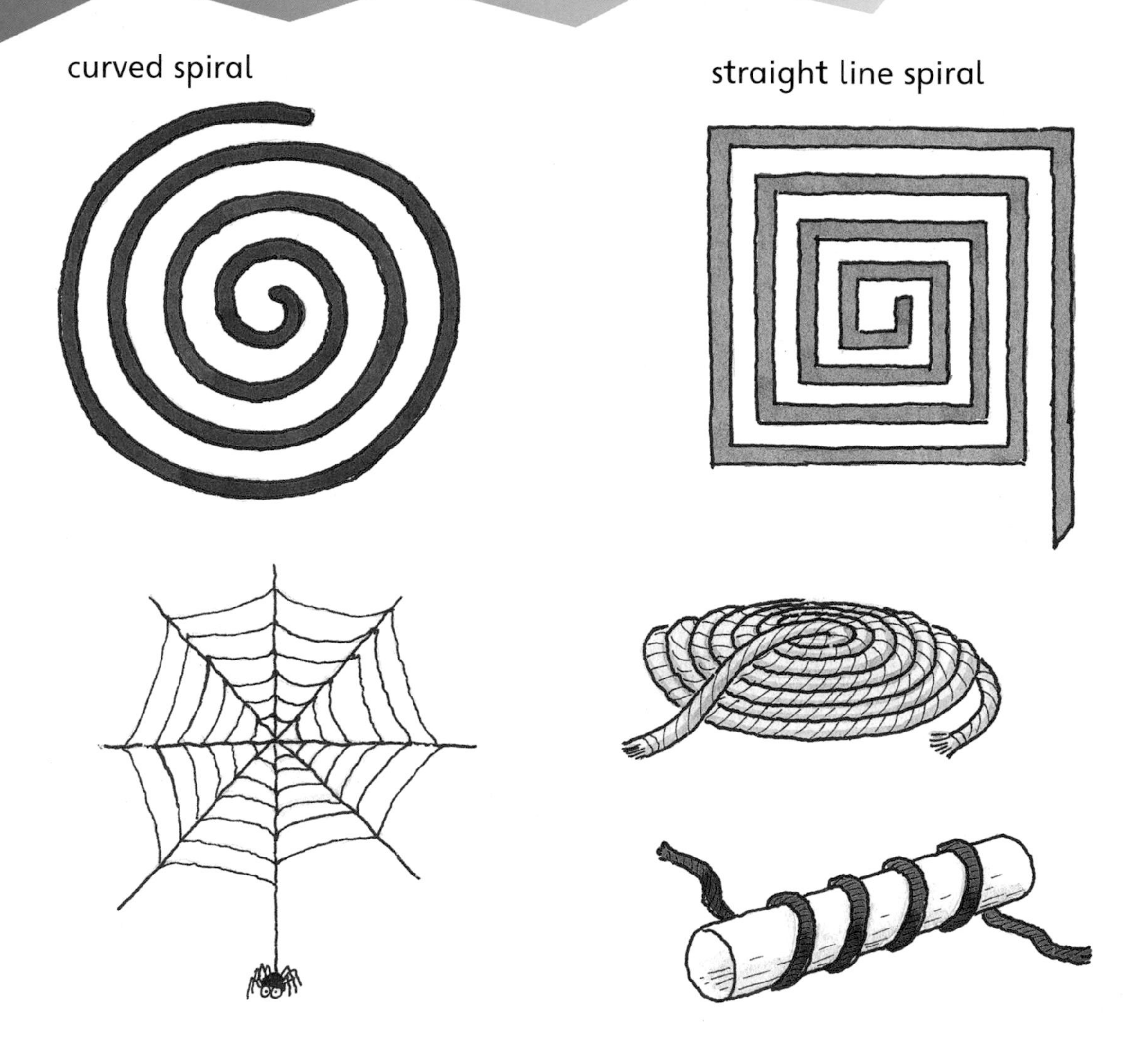

Some **spirals** are lines which wind out from the centre. Other spirals wind round and round like the threads of a screw.

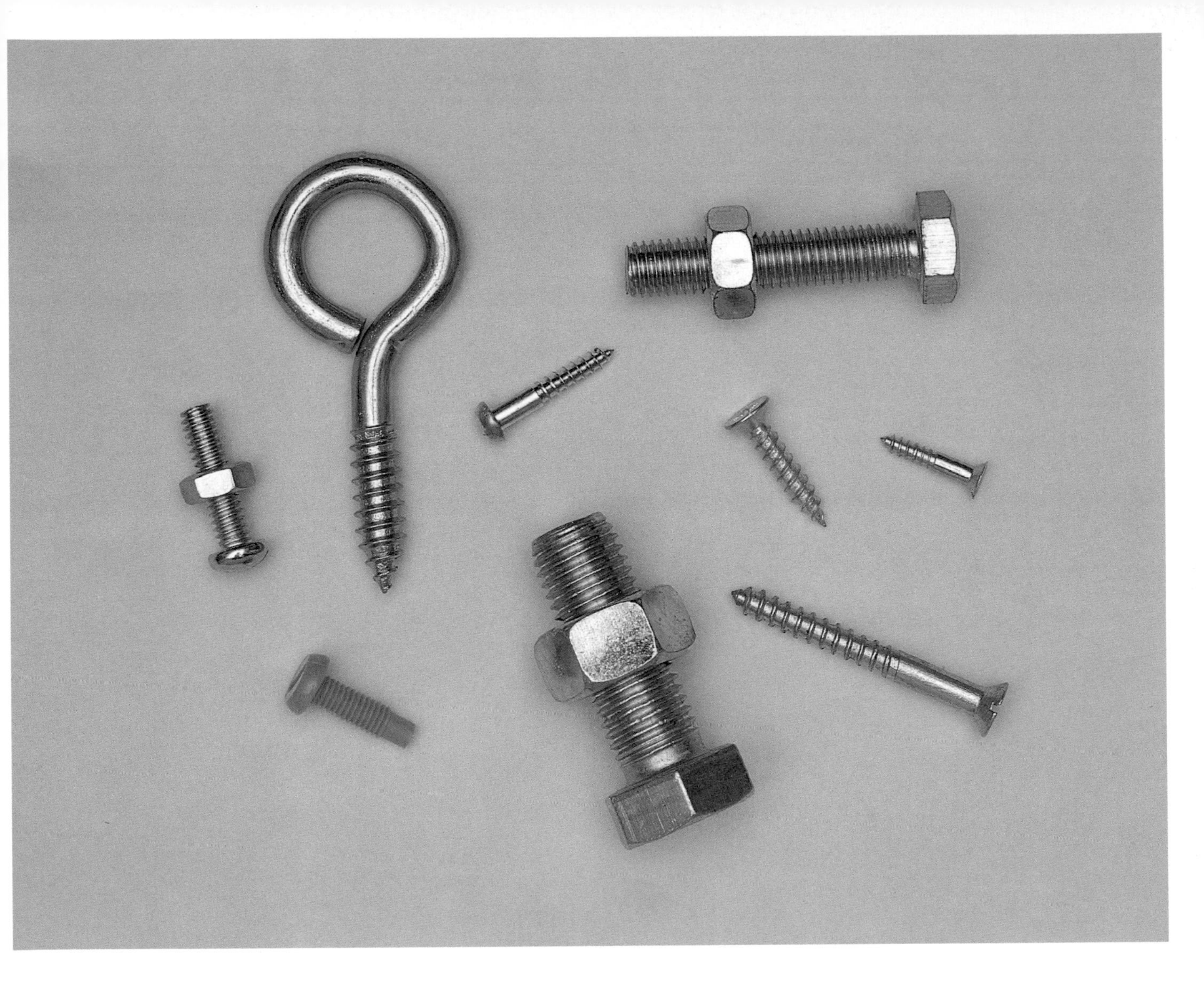

Sometimes the spiral goes to a point like in a wood screw. Sometimes it just **coils** round like on a nut and bolt.

How many spirals can you see in the picture?

Repeating patterns

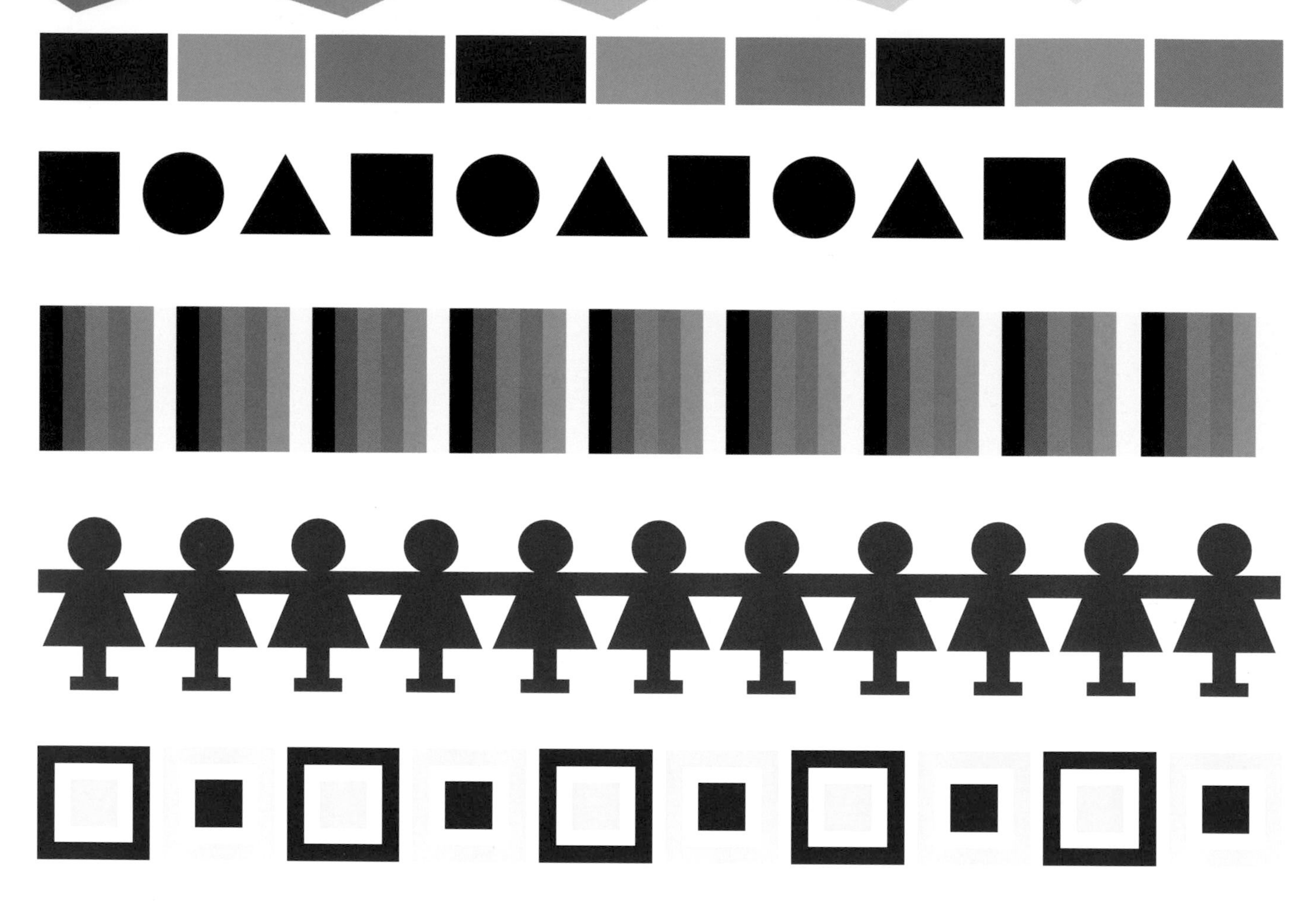

A **sequence** is an order. It can be the order in which something happens. It can also be the order of pictures or objects in a line. Sequences often make **repeating** patterns.

You can see repeating patterns all around you. Sometimes they are natural, and other times people have made them.

Can you see repeating patterns in the picture?

Ring patterns

Some patterns go around in a ring. These are called **ring patterns**. All sorts of things can make ring patterns, such as shapes, colours or lines.

We can find examples of patterns which form a ring all around us. You have to look and see what is being repeated in the patterns.

What are the ring patterns repeated in each one of the pictures above?

Overlapping patterns

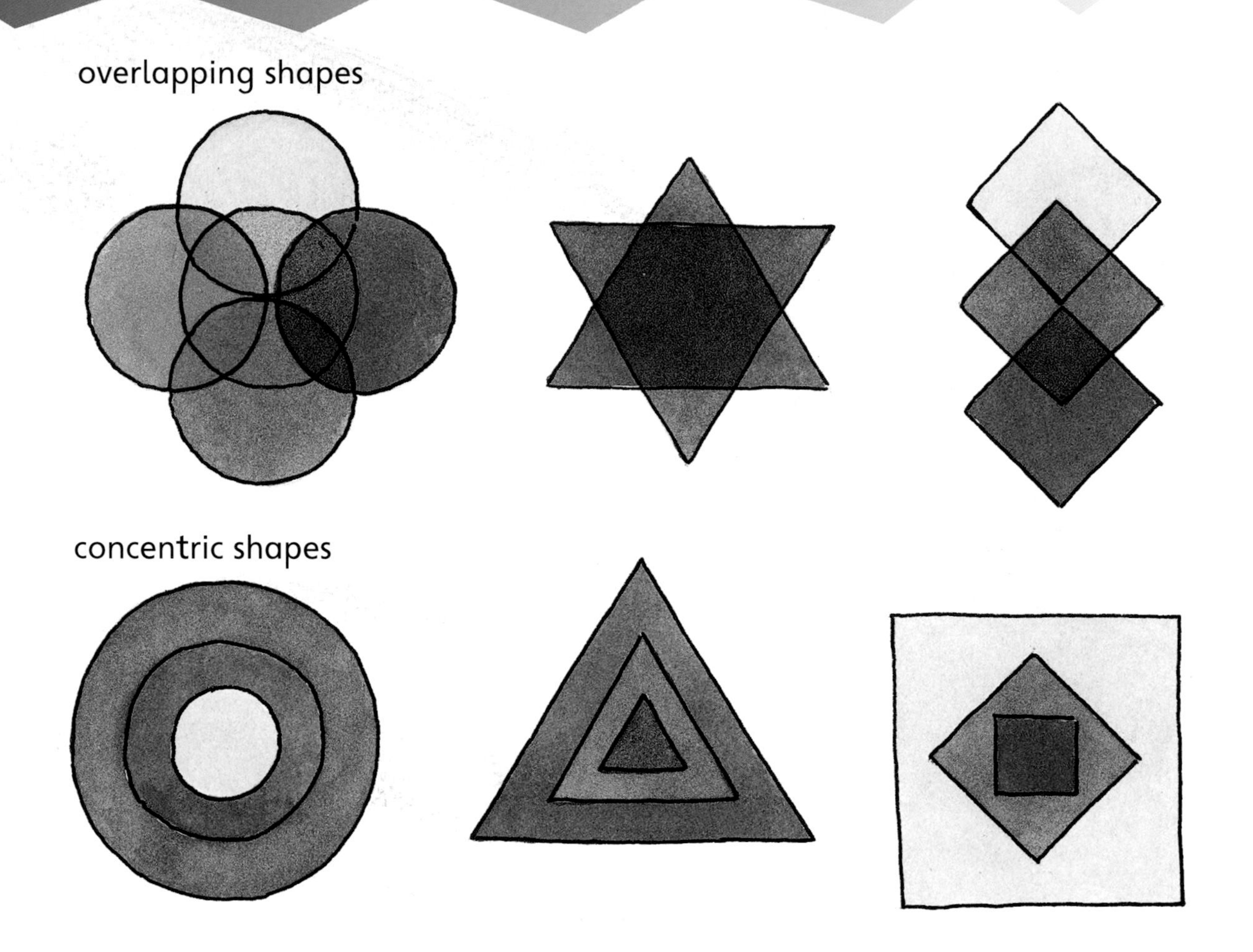

Shapes can **overlap**, or be on top of each other. When they overlap, they often form patterns. Sometimes the centres of the shapes are in the same place. When this happens the shapes are **concentric**.

A bull's-eye target has concentric circles of different colours. The rings on the trunks of cut-down trees are concentric.

Drop a small stone in some water. Can you see the ripples make concentric circles?

Stacking patterns

When people **stack** things, they often arrange them in a pattern. Sometimes the things are stacked tightly, and other times the pattern has gaps.

Builders put their bricks in patterns. They can make many different patterns. Sometimes they make patterns with holes in them.

Look at the photograph. How many different brick patterns can you see in the building?

Number patterns

even

odd

Numbers of things can be arranged to make patterns. An **even number** of things can be arranged in a pattern of twos. An **odd number** of things cannot be arranged in twos.

Arranging something into a pattern makes it easier to count. Often we recognize the pattern and do not have to count.

What are the numbers on these dice? Where else can you see number patterns like these?

Symmetrical patterns

A mirror placed on a coloured paint blot makes a **reflection**. The two halves are the same. The reflection and the design make a **symmetrical** pattern.

There are many symmetrical patterns in nature. The pattern on the right wing of the butterfly is just like the pattern on its left wing.

Can you find other symmetrical patterns around you?

Tessellating patterns

Fitting shapes together without leaving any gaps is called **tessellating**. Sometimes the **tessellation** makes a pattern. A tessellated pattern is sometimes **symmetrical**, but not always.

From earliest times people have made **mosaic** patterns by tessellating with pieces of tile or glass. You may see these patterns on floors, walls, windows and ceilings of important buildings.

Look around your classroom or home. Can you find examples of tessellating patterns?

Glossary

camouflage a disguise which helps something to blend into the background

coil wound round in rings

concentric fitting on top of each other. The centres of the shapes are exactly matched.

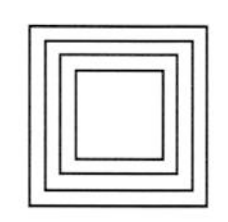 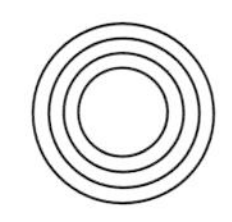

curved lines which are not straight

even numbers numbers of things which can be put into pairs without any left over. 2, 4, 6, 8, 10 are even numbers.

hue a shade of a colour such as dark green or light brown

mosaic pattern made up of small pieces fitted together. A type of tessellation.

odd numbers numbers of things which cannot be put into pairs; there will always be one left over. 1, 3, 5 ,7 ,9 are odd numbers.

overlap something being placed on top of something else

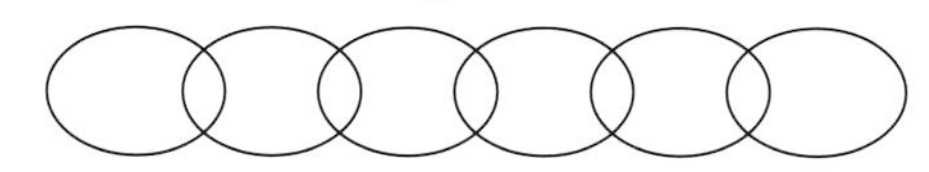

pair two of something

reflection what you see in a mirror

repeating happening more than once

ring patterns a sequence which forms a circle or loop

sequence the order of something. 1 2 2 1 2 2 is a sequence of the numbers 1 and 2.

spiral a line which moves out from a centre. It is often coiled like a spring.

stack arrange 3-D objects tidily, usually on top of each other. 3-D shapes have length, width and thickness or height.

symmetrical a balanced shape or picture. One half is the reflection of the other half.

tessellate fitting shapes together without leaving any gaps

tessellation the pattern made by fitting shapes together without leaving gaps

tint a shade of a colour such as dark blue or light pink

unique nothing else is quite like it

zig-zag moving from side to side in straight lines

Answers

page 5 leopard, tiger, zebra, giraffe, snake

page 7 1 and 5; 2 and 8; 3, 4 and 9; 6 and 7

page 9 bird, horse, dog

page 15 nine

page 19 red and blue beads; round and square beads; short and long petals

page 23 four

page 25 3, 6, 4, 2, 5, 1. Dominoes, playing cards.

Index